DEPARTMENT OF THE NAVY
HEADQUARTERS UNITED STATES MARINE CORPS
3000 MARINE CORPS PENTAGON
WASHINGTON, DC 20350-3000

I0409625

POLICIES AND PROCEDURES FOR ENCROACHMENT CONTROL MANAGEMENT

DEPARTMENT OF THE NAVY
HEADQUARTERS UNITED STATES MARINE CORPS
3000 MARINE CORPS PENTAGON
WASHINGTON, DC 20350-3000

MCO 11011.22B
LFL
27 Jul 2010

MARINE CORPS ORDER 11011.22B

From: Commandant of the Marine Corps
To: Distribution List

Subj: POLICIES AND PROCEDURES FOR ENCROACHMENT CONTROL
        MANAGEMENT

Ref: (a) MCO P5090.2A
        (b) MCO P3550.10
        (c) OPNAVINST 3770.2K
        (d) 10 U.S.C. §2684a
        (e) SECNAVINST 11011.47B
        (f) 16 U.S.C. 1531-1544
        (g) P.L. 108-136, "National Defense Authorization Act
             for Fiscal Year 2004," November 24, 2003
        (h) 16 U.S.C. 670a-670o
        (i) Federal Aviation Administration (FAA) projections for
             2025, February 24, 2009
        (j) P.L. 108-176m: Vision 100 - Century of Aviation (FAA)
             Reauthorization Act," December 12, 2003
        (k) Next Generation Air Transportation System (NGATS)
        (l) White House Office of Science and Technology Policy
             (OSTP), 1976
        (m) Comprehensive Environmental Response, Compensation,
             and Liability Act, December 11, 1980
        (n) 42 U.S.C. §6901
        (o) 33 U.S.C. 26
        (p) 42 U.S.C. 6a
        (q) 6 U.S.C. 31
        (r) 42 U.S.C. 85
        (s) 43 CFR 10
        (t) 16 U.S.C. 470
        (u) 16 U.S.C. 470aa-mm
        (v) 10 U.S.C. §2672

Encl: (1) Policies and Procedures for Encroachment Control
             Management

DISTRIBUTION STATEMENT A: Approved for public release;
distribution is unlimited.

1. <u>Situation</u>. Combat readiness is of the utmost importance to the Marine Corps. In order to achieve the highest levels of readiness, organizations must maintain rigorous and realistic training programs based on approved training standards. Encroachment is a serious threat to the readiness of the Marine Corps. Continued population growth, increased levels of environmental regulations, and incompatible development around military installations, operational ranges, and training areas can create resource (land, air, water, radio frequency spectrum) uses that are incompatible with current and future military testing, training and general mission activities.

2. <u>Cancellation</u>. MCO 11011.22A.

3. <u>Mission</u>. This Order establishes responsibilities for planning, prevention, and control of encroachment.

4. <u>Execution</u>

    a. <u>Commander's Intent and Concept of Operations</u>

        (1) <u>Commander's Intent</u>

           (a) This Order establishes the Deputy Commandant, Installations and Logistics (DC, I&L) as the principal HQMC resource sponsor and Marine Corps proponent for all encroachment control matters.

        (2) <u>Concept of Operations</u>

           (a) The Marine Corps Encroachment Control Program is under the direction of DC, I&L.

           (b) In coordination with Commanding General, Marine Corps Combat Development Command (CG, MCCDC) (C465) and Deputy Commandant, Aviation (DC, AVN), DC, I&L provides Service-wide management and prioritization for planning, prevention, and control of encroachment.

           (c) The Assistant Deputy Commandant, Installations and Logistics (Facilities), (ADC, I&L-LF) is the executive agent for Marine Corps encroachment control policies and programs.

    b. <u>Coordinating Instructions</u>

        (1) Comply with the intent and content of this Order. The terms "shall," "will," and "must" as used in this Order are

directive and require compliance. Words such as "may" and "can" are advisory and do not require compliance.

(2) Submit all recommendations concerning this Order to Commandant of the Marine Corps (CMC (LFL)) via the appropriate chain of command.

5. Administration and Logistics

a. DC, I&L will administer the requirements and ensure the accuracy, modification, and distribution of this Order.

b. Requests for deviations from any of the provisions of this Order must be submitted to Commandant of the Marine Corps CMC (LFL), 2 Navy Annex, Washington, DC 20380-1775.

c. Chapter 1 provides information and guidance on encroachment control responsibilities.

d. Chapter 2 provides information and guidance on encroachment control programs.

e. Chapter 3 provides information and guidance on resourcing encroachment control programs.

f. This Order will be implemented in foreign countries only to the extent the requirements of this Order do not contravene existing Status Of Forces Agreements (SOFAs) and other treaties/executive agreements with a host nation or otherwise contravene mandatory policy guidance issued by a joint command or a sub-unified command.

6. Command and Signal

a. Command. This Order is applicable to the Marine Corps Total Force.

b. Signal. This Order is effective the date signed.

F. PANTER
Deputy Commandant for
Installations and Logistics

Distribution: PCN 10211322600

LOCATOR SHEET

Subj: POLICIES AND PROCEDURES FOR ENCROACHMENT CONTROL

Location:

_____

(Indicate the location(s) of the copy(ies) of this
Order.)

RECORD OF CHANGES

Log completed change action as indicated.

Change Number	Date of Change	Date Entered	Signature of Person Incorporated Change

TABLE OF CONTENTS

TABLE OF CONTENTS

Chapter 1

Responsibilities

1. General. This chapter provides information and guidance on encroachment control responsibilities.

2. Purpose. The purpose of this chapter is to describe responsibilities and authorities pertaining to encroachment control. Effective encroachment control requires an outward-directed, forward-looking, coordinated effort by the entire Marine Corps chain of command. Each level of the Marine Corps hierarchy has responsibilities for assessing current and projected encroachment threats and for engaging other stakeholders in developing effective encroachment control plans and strategies.

3. Deputy Commandant, Installations and Logistics

    a. In addition to the responsibilities outlined in the references, DC, I&L is the proponent for all matters pertaining to the oversight and coordination of encroachment control, including issuing policy and guidance, education, tasking of responsibilities, monitoring accomplishment and resolution of conflicts that may exist with the administration of encroachment control policy and programs.

    b. Assistant Deputy Commandant, Installations and Logistics (Facilities), (ADC, I&L-LF) is the executive agent for encroachment issues within the Marine Corps, coordinates uniform implementation of encroachment control policies and programs, and provides courses of action and recommendations to DC, I&L when regional-level resolution of an encroachment control issue cannot be attained.

    c. Headquarters Marine Corps (HQMC) Facilities Branch (LFF) is the central point of contact on all Marine Corps facilities, infrastructure and Major Repair (M2) and Minor Construction (R2) projects associated with operational ranges and training areas, and coordinates with CG, MCCDC (C465) for application of associated Facility Sustainment Model (FSM) facility condition codes to guide decisions on the use of Operations & Maintenance Marine Corps (O&MMC) funds for operational range and training area facilities.

    d. HQMC Land Use and Military Construction Branch (LFL) serves as the branch-level point of contact for encroachment control and land use and represents the Marine Corps at Department of Defense, joint, and interservice-level meetings pertaining to encroachment.

(1) LFL-1 (Conservation Section) establishes policy and programs related to natural and cultural resources, and the National Environmental Policy Act (NEPA).

(2) LFL-2 (Facilities Planning and Real Estate Section) in coordination with CG, MCCDC (C465) and DC, AVN, formulates, reviews, and executes policies, plans, and programs related to current and future force structure basing, installation facilities requirements, land use requirements plans and studies. LFL-2 is the HQMC section responsible for encroachment policy and programs related to real property acquisition, management, disposal; compatible resource use; encroachment partnering; community planning and outreach; and noise complaint management. Additional responsibilities include the following tasks:

(a) Establish and maintain Marine Corps encroachment control policies and procedures, centrally managed encroachment control budgets, recurring encroachment assessments, military mission sustainment awards program, and coordinate encroachment training and education initiatives.

(b) Participate in partnerships with national-level conservation, development, and public management organizations to promote compatible resource use planning.

(c) Develop, maintain, and update as required, a Marine Corps Encroachment Control Campaign Plan to provide enterprise-wide direction for planning, preparation and execution of the full range of tasks necessary to achieve readiness such that the mission capability of Marine Corps installations, operational ranges, and training areas are fully capable of providing for current and future testing, training and general mission activities.

(d) In coordination with CG, MCCDC (C465) and DC, P&R, develop, maintain, and update as required, an encroachment control programmatic strategy to support the Marine Corps installations vision and the Mission Capable Ranges program tenets of Marine Corps Operational Training Ranges Required Capabilities.

(e) In accordance with reference (d), evaluate, submit and sponsor proposed Marine Corps encroachment partnering projects and funding requests to the Assistant Secretary of the Navy (ASN) for Energy, Installations & Environment (EI&E) and to the Office of the Secretary of Defense (OSD).

(f) Review and approve encroachment partnering projects funded by HQMC Centrally Managed Programs.

(g) Serve as a co-chair (with CG, MCCDC (C465)) on HQMC Working Groups in support of Mission Capable Ranges.

(h) Maintain this Order and update as required.

(3) LFL-3 (Asset Utilization Section) coordinates all actions related to real property asset accountability, and geospatial and facilities data.

(4) LFL-4 (MILCON Program Section) coordinates with CG, MCCDC (C465) for prioritization of Military Construction (MILCON) and requirements for operational ranges, training area enhancements and projects; and coordinates with Commander, Marine Forces Reserve (Deputy, Assistant Chief of Staff Facilities) for prioritization of Military Construction Naval Reserve (Marine Corps specific) requirements for reserve facility projects.

(5) LFL-5 (Environmental Management Section) establishes policy and manages programs related to environmental compliance, pollution prevention and environmental restoration to include munitions response on closed ranges.

4. Commanding General, Marine Corps Combat Development Command (CG, MCCDC) (C465))

a. In addition to the responsibilities outlined in reference (b), Commanding General, Marine Corps Combat Development Command (CG, MCCDC (C465)) is the proponent for all matters pertaining to the oversight and coordination of operational ranges and training areas, including issuing policy and guidance as the executive agent for ranges and training area issues within the Marine Corps.

b. Director, Range and Training Area Management Division (C465) serves as the Service single point of contact for all range and training area management issues and represents the Marine Corps at DOD, joint, and interservice-level meetings pertaining to range and training areas. Serve as a co-chair (with CMC LFL-3) on HQMC Working Groups in support of Mission Capable Ranges.

c.   In coordination with CMC (LFL) and DC, P&R, develop, maintain, and update as required, an encroachment control programmatic strategy to support the Marine Corps installations vision and the Mission Capable Ranges program tenets of Marine Corps Operational Training Ranges Required Capabilities.

5.   Deputy Commandant, Aviation (DC, AVN)

a.   In addition to the responsibilities outlined in references (b) and (c), DC, AVN is the principal HQMC resource sponsor and Marine Corps proponent for planning, prevention, and control of encroachment in associated special use airspace.

b.   Coordinate and monitor with CG, MCCDC (C465) and CMC (LFL) on Marine Corps Special Use Airspace issues, proposed range training area projects that require changes to existing airspace or air traffic control procedures to ensure compatibility with other aviation requirements, and aviation weapons and ammunition procurement as they pertain to range and training area requirements.

c.   Provide representation to HQMC Working Groups in support of Mission Capable Ranges.

6.   Deputy Commandant, Programs and Resources (DC, P&R)

a.   In coordination with CMC (LFL) and CG, MCCDC (C465), develop an enterprise-wide encroachment control Planning, Programming, Budgeting, and Execution (PPBE) strategy to support the Marine Corps installations vision and the Mission Capable Ranges program tenets of Marine Corps Operational Training Ranges Required Capabilities.

b.   Provide representation to HQMC Working Groups in support of Mission Capable Ranges.

7.   Deputy Commandant, Plans, Policies and Operations (DC, PP&O)

a.   In coordination with CG, MCCDC (C465) and CMC (LFL), participate in the staff coordination of operational matters, MAGTF matters, combat readiness, security matters, amphibious and pre-positioning matters related to the planning, prevention, and control of encroachment.

b. Provide representation to HQMC Working Groups in support of Mission Capable Ranges.

8. <u>Deputy Commandant, Manpower and Reserve Affairs (DC, MR&A)</u>. In coordination with CG, MCCDC (C465) and CMC (LFL), participate in the staff coordination of personnel matters related to the planning, prevention, and control of encroachment.

9. <u>Counsel for the Commandant (CL)</u>

a. CL will assist CG, MCCDC (C465) and CMC (LFL), by providing land use, environmental, and procurement law guidance on encroachment issues affecting the Marine Corps.

b. CL, through the Field and Area Counsel Offices, will provide legal support in matters under the Counsel's primary cognizance including land use, environmental, and procurement law.

c. Provide representation to HQMC Working Groups in support of Mission Capable Ranges.

10. <u>Director, Public Affairs (PA)</u>

a. In coordination with CMC (LFL), establish and maintain Marine Corps message objectives and Questions and Answers (Q&As), pertinent to the policies and procedures in this Order, for public affairs purposes, to include installation programs, community relations, media relations and internal relations.

b. Engage national, regional, and local media outlets to inform the public of the Marine Corps mission needs and encroachment issues.

c. Liaise with DOD Public Affairs (Marine Corps account holder).

d. Provide representation to HQMC Working Groups in support of Mission Capable Ranges.

11. <u>Director, Office of Legislative Affairs (OLA)</u>

a. In coordination with CMC (LFL), establish and maintain a federal legislative monitoring process pertinent to the policies and procedures in this Order.

b.   In coordination with CMC (LFL) and CL, develop, propose, and support legislative, regulatory, and administrative initiatives pertinent to the policies and procedures in this Order.

12.   <u>Inspector General of the Marine Corps (IGMC)</u>.   In coordination with CMC (LFL), establish and maintain an encroachment control program assessment process to promote Marine Corps combat readiness, integrity, efficiency, effectiveness, and credibility for sustainment of Marine Corps installations military mission.

13.   <u>Commanding General, Marine Corps Systems Command (CG, MCSC)</u>

a.   Program Manager, Training Systems (TRASYS), coordinate with CG, MCCDC (C465) and CMC (LFL) to identify, validate, and coordinate the submission of Range and Training Area Program Objective Memorandum (POM) initiatives and procurement costs associated with range and training area MILCON projects, fielding of range training equipment, and for the requirements and policies per reference (b).

b.   Develop system profiles that can be used for assessment of future mission impacts, preparation of pollution prevention plans, and preparation of NEPA documents.

c.   Provide representation to HQMC Working Groups in support of Mission Capable Ranges.

14.   <u>Commanders, Marine Corps Forces Commands</u>

a.   Review and endorse strategies, studies and plans that respond to current and future encroachment threats from both inside the installation and between the installation and the community that adversely affect or have the potential to adversely affect Marine Corps installations, operational ranges, training areas, associated special use airspace, and other locations where the Marine Corps trains within the respective geographic or functional Area of Responsibility (AOR).

b.   Provide subordinate operational force commanders with assistance in identifying future training requirements that may require additional encroachment control resources.

15. <u>Commanding Generals, Marine Corps Installations (CG,
MCI) and Commanding Generals, Marine Corps Recruit Depots,
Commander, Marine Corps Base Quantico</u>

a. Exercise overall responsibility for coordinating Marine
Corps encroachment control strategies within respective region.

b. For MCI's, establish a Region Community Plans and
Liaison Office to serve as the primary point of contact to
coordinate region-wide implementation of encroachment control
plans and programs referenced in this Order.

c. For MCI's, develop a Region Encroachment Control Plan
(ECP) as the operational-level plan to support the Marine Corps'
overall encroachment control strategy in the white-space. Once
established, maintain and update.

d. For MCI's, establish and maintain a region-wide
encroachment control programmatic strategy to support Marine
Expeditionary Force commanders Training Exercise and Employment
Plan (TEEP). Specifically, review management actions generated
from the Region ECP process to make program decisions on
functional POM submissions.

e. Monitor political, environmental, social, economic,
governmental and administrative matters at the regional level in
developing encroachment control strategies.

f. In coordination with CMC (LFL) and OLA, establish and
maintain an engagement process with regional and state elected
officials and staffs to achieve situational awareness of
proposed resource (land, air, water, radio frequency spectrum)
use changes and initiatives that have the potential to impact
military activities within the white-space.

g. For MCI's, in coordination with CMC (LFL), coordinate
state- and regional-level encroachment control initiatives with
public officials and conservators within respective region.

h. In coordination with CG, MCCDC (C465), ensure that
actions affecting existing airspace procedures or areas are
properly planned and processed through the Regional Airspace
Coordinators and Command Airspace Liaison Officers for effective
scheduling, utilization, and protection of special use airspace
within respective region.

i. Identify, prioritize, and support installation requirements for range and training areas and range training equipment within respective region or training command.

j. For MCI's analyze and rank order encroachment partnering project proposals submitted by installations within respective region and forward region consolidated recommendations to CMC (LFL). MCRD's and MCB Quantico analyze and rank order encroachment partnering proposals and submit to CMC (LFL).

k. Maintain contact with other Services equivalent commands and other military land-holding activities within the respective mission area or region to exchange information on encroachment and compatible resource use planning practices.

16. Commanders, Marine Corps Bases and Stations

a. Exercise overall responsibility for implementation of respective Marine Corps installation encroachment control program.

b. Establish an Installation Community Plans and Liaison Office to serve as the primary point of contact to coordinate and manage installation-wide implementation of encroachment control plans and programs referenced in this Order.

c. Develop an Installation ECP as the tactical-level plan to support the Marine Corps' overall encroachment control strategy both internal to the installation and the surrounding area inclusive of installation range compatibility zones (or study planning areas). Once established, maintain and update.

d. Establish and maintain an installation encroachment control programmatic strategy to support tenant Major Subordinate Command (MSC) commanders TEEP. Specifically, review management actions generated from the Installation ECP process to make program decisions on functional POM submissions.

e. Monitor political, environmental, social, economic, governmental and administrative matters at the local level in developing encroachment control strategies.

f. Establish and maintain an outreach and engagement process with local elected officials and staffs and community stakeholders to achieve situational awareness of proposed resource (land, air, water, radio frequency spectrum) use changes and initiatives that have the potential to impact military activities internal to the installation and the surrounding area inclusive of installation range compatibility zones (or study planning areas).

g. Coordinate installation-level encroachment control initiatives that involve public officials and conservators within local area of interest with CG, MCI of respective region.

h. Ensure adherence with applicable federal, state, and local environmental and MILCON submission requirements per reference (a).

17. Commanders, Operational Forces

a. Operational Force commanders and training coordinators will review TEEP resource (land, air, water, radio frequency spectrum) requirements with appropriate Region- and Installation-level commander and staff on a recurrent basis, to identify associated encroachment issues that have the potential to impact military activities internal to the installation and the surrounding area inclusive of installation range compatibility zones (or study planning areas) and within the white-space.

b. Operational Force commanders and training coordinators should consider the impact of future military activities (basing and employment of new weapons systems and associated tactics, techniques and procedures), resources (land, air, water, radio frequency spectrum), and use training requirements with appropriate Region- and Installation-level commanders and staffs on a recurrent basis, in order to identify associated encroachment issues that have the potential to impact military activities internal to the installation and the surrounding area inclusive of installation range compatibility zones (or study planning areas) and within the white-space.

18. Headquarters, Marine Corps Mission Capable Ranges Working Group

a. The purpose of the HQMC Mission Capable Ranges Working Group is to develop encroachment control strategies and implementation plans that fulfill the Marine Corps installations vision and the Mission Capable Ranges program tenets of Marine Corps Operational Training Ranges Required Capabilities.

b. The mission of the HQMC Mission Capable Ranges Working Group is to act as the HQMC coordinating body responsible for oversight, development, and coordination of a comprehensive Marine Corps response to encroachment pressures that adversely affect or have the potential to adversely affect Marine Corps installations, operational ranges, training areas, associated special use airspace, sea space, radio frequency spectrum and other locations where the Marine Corps conducts current and plans future military testing, training and general mission activities.

c. CG, MCCDC (C465) establishes Service-level range and training area spatial requirements and capabilities from established training requirements while CMC (LF) provides facilities, natural and cultural resources management, planning, real estate, environmental compliance, and land use related policies, plans, and programs for integration into an overall military mission sustainment strategy of Marine Corps installations, operational ranges and training areas.

Chapter 2

Programs

1. General. This chapter provides information and guidance on encroachment control programs.

2. Purpose. The purpose of this chapter is to describe strategies and establish procedures pertaining to encroachment control. Effective encroachment control requires Marine Corps leaders to understand that continued population growth, increased levels of environmental regulations, and incompatible development around military installations, operational ranges, and training areas can create resource (land, air, water, radio frequency spectrum) uses that are incompatible with current and future military testing, training and general mission activities.

3. Encroachment Control Team

    a. Region and Installation commanders must promote and sustain the concepts of outreach and long-term collaborative planning and problem solving with stakeholders to ensure compatible resource use within their respective zones of engagement.

    b. Region and Installation commanders may establish and maintain an Encroachment Control Team from within existing staffs.

    c. Members of the Encroachment Control Team may include among others: Community Plans and Liaison Office; planning, facilities, and real estate managers; environmental, natural and cultural resources program managers; range and training area managers; airspace coordinators; general counsel; public affairs; major tenant commands and operational forces representatives.

    d. Region and Installation Encroachment Control Team responsibilities include:

    (1) Assist the commander in the discharge of encroachment control responsibilities.

    (2) Establish personnel requirements and maintain staff to implement and manage encroachment control program activities.

    (3) Coordinate review of and develop positions for the commander to proposed federal, state or local agency legislation, regulations, guidelines, programs, plans or other documents

relevant to encroachment. Pertinent subject matter includes environmental documentation, resource use planning documents, or other studies and analyses.

(4) Review and evaluate proposals, including lease agreements, received from any non-DOD activity seeking use of installation real property to avoid actual or potential impact to training and other mission activities internal to the installation.

(5) The Region and Installation Community Plans and Liaison Office should be designated as the staff member responsible to coordinate the functioning of the respective Encroachment Control Team.

4. Community Plans and Liaison Office (CPLO)

a. The Marine Corps focal point for implementing compatible resource use planning and coordinating outreach for encroachment control is the Community Plans and Liaison Office.

b. The (CPLO) Community Plans and Liaison Office is the Marine Corps staff member responsible to conduct outreach; monitor and assess encroachment activities and incompatible resource (land, air, water, radio frequency spectrum) uses that could adversely impact current and future military testing, training and general mission activities on Marine Corps installations, operational ranges, and training areas.

c. The CPLO is most effective if working directly for the Base Commander in a senior position. Commanders are encouraged to delegate a wide range of authority in representing the command in the public forum and managing the encroachment control program.

d. Region and Installation Community Plans and Liaison Office responsibilities include:

(1) Consistent with sustainment of bases and stations military mission, integrate the encroachment control plan with the applicable Integrated Natural Resources Management Plan (INRMP), Integrated Cultural Resources Management Plan (ICRMP), compatible resource use studies and analyses and other associated region and installation planning activities to support operations and training requirements.

(2) Serve as the primary point of contact for encroachment concerns and issues during planning and

implementation of a comprehensive resource use management program.

(3) Develop and maintain a network with elected and appointed officials at the federal, state, regional, and local levels to promote current and future military activities on Marine Corps installations and within the white-space.

(4) Actively participate in the public comment and review process for community development plans to promote compatible resource use planning goals. CPLO's are encouraged to participate on local and regional planning councils, water and sewer boards, transportation committees, etc. (Ex-Officio) as a means to maintain earliest awareness of incompatible development, and to create working relationships with community leaders, planners and governing bodies.

(5) Develop and maintain working relationships with state, regional and local conservation agencies and private conservation organizations by participating in conservation forums led by state or local conservation agencies or private conservation organizations.

(6) Conduct outreach to educate the public regarding the importance of the installation and its ability to support military activities to sustain a combat ready Marine Corps.

(7) Participate in community events to raise public awareness of the installations environmental management role, the mutual benefits of compatible resource use planning, and the economic contributions the installation provides the community.

(8) Implement encroachment control plans and programs referenced in this Order.

(9) In coordination with the Encroachment Control Team, participate in and monitor the development of installation master plans, development plans, facility siting approvals and construction design initiatives to ensure that the negative effects of internal encroachment from suburbanization (sprawl) and the construction of incompatible structures are minimized to ensure sustainment of bases and stations military mission. This requirement may be enhanced by participation on the Installation Environmental Review Board (EIRB).

5. Region Encroachment Control Plan

a. Region commanders will develop a Region Encroachment Control Plan as the operational-level plan to support the Marine Corps' overall encroachment control strategy in the white-space.

b. The composition of a Region Encroachment Control Plan typically includes elements common to Installation Encroachment Control Plans but primarily addresses encroachment issues and associated training impact factors of concern in the white-space.

6. Installation Encroachment Control Plan

a. Base and Station commanders will develop an Installation ECP as the tactical-level plan to support the Marine Corps' overall encroachment control strategy both internal to the installation and the surrounding area inclusive of installation range compatibility zones (or study planning areas).

b. The intent of the Encroachment Control Plan is to reduce the negative effects of encroachment on operations and training such that Marine Corps installations, operational ranges, and training areas are fully capable of supporting current and future testing, training and general mission activities.

c. The purpose of the Encroachment Control Plan is to comprehensively identify current and future encroachment threats from both inside the installation and between the installation and the community, develop a suite of appropriate options for effectively addressing encroachment issues, develop a proactive joint installation and community action plan to implement high priority encroachment management actions, and aid in developing and sustaining community and stakeholder planning relationships.

d. An ECP is generally divided into six major sections of which four are made public. The four sections of the ECP to be shared publicly are: Introduction, Community Analysis, Mission Analysis, and Action Plan. The Encroachment Management and Acquisition Strategy and the Strategic Communications Plan are the fifth and sixth major sections of an Encroachment Control Plan and are For Official Use Only (FOUO) internal to DOD.

(1) The introduction section identifies the purpose, scope and organization of the ECP.

(2) The community analysis section identifies the economic, social, governance, and planning frameworks that the installation exists within at the local, regional, and state levels.

(3) The mission analysis section benchmarks the installation's mission against encroachment issues currently used to assess installations, operational ranges, training areas and associated airspace and the set of encroachment associated training impacts.

(4) The action plan creates specific implementation strategies for each of the selected best-fit encroachment management options. Individual actions are sequenced and time phased, and implementation responsibilities are specified. The action plan provides the commander with metrics to monitor progress in achieving the installation's encroachment management objectives.

(5) The encroachment management and acquisition strategy is the fifth major section of an ECP that provides the installation an internal, For Official Use Only (FOUO) plan of potential land acquisitions for buffer purposes, discussions on internal encroachment, and discussions on issues and actions that require higher headquarters' actions that may be of a sensitive nature.

(6) The Strategic Communications Plan (SCP) is the sixth major section of an ECP that provides the installation commander a process and roadmap for engaging stakeholders. The SCP helps guide implementation of the ECP Action Plan, formulation of conservation forums and development of stakeholder relationships.

e. Mission impacts are identified through a review of existing studies and plans and by interviewing installation training providers, service support providers, and anti-terrorism and force protection staffs. The set of installation-specific encroachment issues identified in the mission analysis is evaluated against practices and tools that are available to the installation to aid in correcting, minimizing, and preventing the impacts. The suite of potential options for addressing encroachment problems is then evaluated, in conjunction with installation staff, on the basis of effectiveness, cost, appropriateness, and other parameters to identify the best-fit encroachment management options for implementation.

7. Outreach and Engagement Plan

a. To further the purpose of the Region and Installation ECP strategies, Region, Base and Station commanders will each develop an Outreach and Engagement Plan to include Public Affairs, Media Affairs, Legislative Affairs and Community Relations functions. Once established, maintain and update.

b. The Region and Installation Community Plans and Liaison Office should be designated as the staff member responsible to coordinate the functioning of the outreach and engagement plan.

c. The purpose of an Outreach and Engagement plan is to communicate to stakeholders, the importance of the installation's military mission, contribution to military readiness and national defense, and the threat posed by encroachment.

d. Elements of the Outreach and Engagement plan include the overarching Service message, command specific messages, and public affairs, media affairs, legislative affairs and community relations actions that support the overarching Service- and command specific message objectives. Once established, maintain and update.

e. Action required to implement an effective Outreach and Engagement plan includes establishment of the following proactive programs:

(1) Outreach, as discussed in this Order, refers to the process of communicating through mutual dialogue and information exchange to inform and educate stakeholders about current and future military testing, training and general mission activities on Marine Corps installations, operational ranges, and training areas.

(2) Stakeholders, as discussed in this Order, refer to a person or organization having a personal or financial interest in an issue or decision. Stakeholders include DOD personnel, individuals or groups external to DOD, current and future land owners, local or national activist groups, non-governmental organizations (NGOs), local and state governments and the media.

(3) Engagement, as discussed in this Order, refers to the process of facilitating collaboration among internal and external entities to find common ground among diverse interests in order to reach mutually acceptable solutions to complex military mission sustainment issues.

(a) Public Affairs, in coordination with the Director, Public Affairs (HQMC), establish and maintain Marine Corps Public Affairs Guidance pertinent to the policies and procedures in this plan, to include regional and installation programs, community relations, media relations, and internal relations.

(b) Media Affairs engages national, regional, and local media outlets to inform the public of the Marine Corps military mission sustainment needs and encroachment issues. Establish a CPLO link on the command's web page. Engage corporate and non-governmental organizations (NGOs) to inform the public of the Marine Corps military mission sustainment needs and encroachment issues.

(c) Legislative Affairs develops and maintains a network with elected and appointed officials at the federal, state, regional, and local levels to provide information about current and future military testing, training and general mission activities on Marine Corps installations, operational ranges, training areas, and within the white-space.

(4) Community Relations, as discussed in this Order, refers to the process of open, ongoing, two-way dialogue between DOD and public stakeholders that proactively seeks and considers stakeholder input, addresses issues that may affect the public, develops sound and reasonable proposals, and disseminates informational and educational materials to inform the public about current and future military testing, training and general mission activities on Marine Corps installations, operational ranges, and training areas.

(a) Conduct outreach to educate the public regarding the value and importance of the installation and its capability and capacity requirements to support current and future military testing, training and general mission activities to sustain a combat ready Marine Corps.

(b) Participate in community events to raise public awareness of the installation's environmental management role, the mutual benefits of long-term collaborative planning to ensure compatible resource use, and the economic contributions the installation provides the community.

(c) Participate, communicate, build relationships and share information with stakeholders that may include establishing publically accessible electronic mediums such as websites to ensure current and future military testing, training and general mission activities needs are articulated.

   (5) General

     (a) Develop and maintain working relationships with state, regional and local conservation agencies and private conservation organizations by participating in state and local conservation forums.

     (b) Actively participate in the public comment and review process for community development plans to promote compatible resource use planning goals.

     (c) Develop and maintain working relationships with energy working groups, agencies and private organizations and participate in state, local and DOD energy resource planning initiatives that could impact Special Use Airspace, Military Training Routes, and use of range and training areas.

8. Compatible Resource Use Studies and Analyses. Implementation of encroachment control activities provides for compatible resource use as described in the purpose statements of the following programs.

  a. The purpose of the Air Installation Compatible Use Zones (AICUZ) program is to provide local communities tools required to identify land uses compatible with noise levels, accident potential and obstruction clearance criteria associated with military airfield operations.

  b. The purpose of the Range Air Installation Compatible Use Zones (RAICUZ) program is to provide local communities tools required to identify land uses that will be compatible with noise levels and range compatibility zones associated with military aviation range operations.

  c. The purpose of the Range Compatible Use Zones (RCUZ) program is to provide local communities tools required to identify land uses that will be compatible with noise levels and range compatibility zones associated with military aviation range and/or military ground range operations.

  d. The purpose of the Joint Land Use Study (JLUS) is to provide a cooperative land planning process to assist communities near military installations or ranges to develop initiatives that help mitigate military impacts on community resources. The JLUS is sponsored by DOD Office of Economic

Adjustment (OEA) to promote planned development compatible with the training and operational mission of the military installation or range.

9. Encroachment Partnering

a. Congress responded to the military departments' request for encroachment control assistance in 2003 by enacting reference (d). This authority allows the Services to enter into Encroachment Partnering (EP) agreements with state and local governments, agencies and private organizations to acquire interests in real property in the vicinity of, or ecologically related to, military installations, operational ranges or military airspace for purposes of:

(1) Limiting development or use of property that would be incompatible with the mission of the installation, or

(2) Preserving habitat in a manner that would relieve environmental restrictions on military training, testing, or operations on the installation.

b. Assistant Secretary of the Navy, Energy, Installations and Environment, (ASN,EI&E) provides overall policy for encroachment management for DON, and provides prior approval of agreements under this authority.

c. Per reference (e), with the prior approval of CMC, Commander, Naval Facilities Engineering Command (COMNAVFACENGCOM) has the delegated authority to execute agreements and real estate transactions under this authority.

d. CMC (LFL-2) provides encroachment control program oversight, coordinates policy with ASN, I&E and COMNAVFACENGCOM, develops EP project submittal and review criteria, pursues funding for EP projects, and provides support to region and installation EP program planning and development.

e. Encroachment Partnering is a key component of the Marine Corps' encroachment control strategy. The Marine Corps follows several guiding principles when exercising this authority:

(1) The overarching goal of encroachment control is to ensure the integrity of current and future military testing, training and general mission activities on Marine Corps installations, operational ranges, and training areas. In implementing that goal, the Marine Corps will give due consideration to conserving natural resources and to promoting

the productive, compatible use of land in the vicinity of Marine Corps installations.

(2) Encroachment partnering leverages the shared interest and financial ability of the Marine Corps and partner organizations to restrict incompatible development and preserve habitat near installations. The Marine Corps will pursue partnerships where each party provides an equitable contribution and receives valuable consideration for their participation.

(3) Encroachment Partnering relies on the mutual efforts of many parties. The Marine Corps will seek the best project proposals from all eligible sources and will avoid the appearance of favoring any potential partner.

(4) Per reference (e), this authority may not be used to acquire land for Marine Corps occupancy, military training or operations. Indirect use (e.g., overflight, noise) is not prohibited.

    f. Two organizational elements which are essential to the EP process are the Conservation Forum and the Encroachment Partnering Acquisition Team (EPAT).

(1) To promote and implement EP programs, the Marine Corps participates in Conservation Forums led by states or non-governmental organizations. The Marine Corps, as a matter of policy, does not lead Conservation Forums. These forums are typically open to all interested federal, state, and local agencies, military Services and non-governmental organizations and individuals. Though not required, a charter agreed to by all participants often governs forum activities.

(a) The purpose of a Conservation Forum is to identify mutually agreeable criteria for land acquisition, identify land available for acquisition, develop a real estate process that meets all participants' legal requirements for property acquisition, and bring together interested members of the forum to conduct real estate transactions.

(b) Generally, a Conservation Forum project work effort is comprised of three categories: (1) criteria development and property identification, (2) political support, and (3) real estate transaction.

<u>1</u>. Criteria development and property identification work groups bring a wealth of ecological and social knowledge of landscapes that are vital to ensuring

effective use of the encroachment partnering authority. These groups include universities, federal and state regulatory agencies, and non-governmental organizations that focus on ecosystem health.

  <u>2</u>. Organizations that provide political support are those who garner support and influence opinions of relevant constituencies. These organizations include national and local land use, environmental and conservation groups.

  <u>3</u>. Real estate transaction partners are those who directly participate in real estate acquisitions. These groups typically include the military Services, state and local government agencies and national and local land trusts.

  (2) The EPAT is comprised of installation and/or MCI subject matter experts such as Community Plans and Liaison Office, Natural Resources, Real Estate and Facilities staff, as well as representatives from NAVFAC and HQMC. The EPAT is responsible for EP planning, project development, acquisition strategy, funding, and execution actions. The installation or MCI CPLO will typically lead the EPAT.

  g. Encroachment Partnering may not satisfy all encroachment-related real estate requirements, especially those involving high-cost property, properties involving a reluctant seller, or properties for which a funding partner is not able to be found.

  (1) In some cases, Military Construction (MILCON) or minor land acquisition authorities may be a more appropriate means of acquisition.

  (2) Acquisition may not be possible in all cases. Other encroachment control measures should also be pursued concurrently in an overarching encroachment control strategy, including working with local and state officials to ensure that development controls and habitat preservation initiatives take military requirements into consideration.

Chapter 3

Resources

1. <u>General</u>. This chapter provides information and guidance on resourcing encroachment control programs.

2. <u>Purpose</u>. The purpose of this chapter is to describe procedures pertaining to resourcing encroachment control programs. Effective encroachment control requires a coordinated strategy that resources to the total set of requirements and establishes a program of record which meets CMC objectives and achieves readiness such that the mission capability of Marine Corps Installations, operational ranges, and training areas are fully capable of providing for current and future testing, training and general mission activities.

3. <u>Programming</u>

   a. Support for funding requirements is provided through the Program Objective Memorandum (POM) and Offices of the Secretary of Defense, Secretary of Navy, and CMC programmatic guidance.

   b. Project types addressed in this chapter include O&MMC (Operations & Maintenance Marine Corps) appropriation including minor land acquisitions and encroachment partnering projects (EP). As used in this Order, the term "minor land acquisition" means the acquisition of interests in land which can be acquired within the authority of HQMC and EP project acquisitions pursuant to reference (v), as amended, and is not subject to acquisition under the authority of an annual military construction (MILCON) program.

   c. Project types excluded from the provisions of this chapter are those funded from Procurement, Marine Corps (PMC) appropriation, Research, Development, Test and Evaluation (RDT&E) appropriation and regular MILCON.

4. <u>Real Estate and Encroachment Control Centrally Managed Program Funds</u>

   a. Prior to the beginning of a fiscal year, CMC (LFL) issues an annual program status report request and Real Estate and Encroachment Control project requirement funding request data call. The purpose of the annual program status report is for Marine Corps Training Commands, Regions and Installations to identify the posture of their respective encroachment control programs. The purpose of the project requirement funding

request data call is for training commands, regions and
installations to identify budget year and out-fiscal year real
estate and encroachment control funding requirements to be
supported from HQMC Centrally Managed Program identified for the
Real Estate and Encroachment Control Program.

    b. The Real Estate and Encroachment Control Centrally
Managed Program is comprised of real estate, encroachment
control, and community planning elements.

    c. Requests for funding requirements serve a two-fold
purpose. They are:

        (1) Requests provide detailed data for budget year
projects.

        (2) Installations establish long-range requirements for
the remaining years of the current Future Years Defense Plan
(FYDP).

    d. Requests for HQMC Real Estate and Encroachment Control
Centrally Managed Program funding support within the following
project categories will be associated to management actions
generated from the Training Command, Region or Installation ECP
process. Requests not supported by the ECP process will require
justification.

        (1) Real Property and Land Management Services
identifies Naval Facilities Engineering Command (NAVFACENGCOM)
support and services, such as labor and travel.

        (2) Planning - Minor Land Acquisitions and Encroachment
Partnering projects identifies land planning activities, such as
real estate appraisals, environmental baseline studies,
environmental documentation, boundary surveys, title searches,
and other supporting documentation needed to complete minor land
acquisitions, encroachment partnering acquisitions or other
encroachment control support planning.

        (3) Acquisition - Minor Land Acquisitions and
Encroachment Partnering projects identifies the purchase price,
planning costs, and closing costs for minor land acquisitions
and EP projects.

        (4) Community Plans and Liaison Office Support provides
for the implementation of military mission sustainment
activities, encroachment control planning, and outreach and
engagement strategies for compatible resource use consistent

with the encroachment control plans and programs referenced in this Order.

(5) Compatible Resource Use Strategic Planning includes development of Training Command, Region or Installation Encroachment Control Plans (ECPs), special land use studies, and other real estate and encroachment control issues and deficiencies that address encroaching development and compatible resource use opportunities.

(6) Air Installation Compatible Use Zones (AICUZ) Studies identify land uses compatible with noise levels, accident potential and obstruction clearance criteria associated with military airfield operations.

(7) Range Air Installation Compatible Use Zones (RAICUZ) Studies identify land uses compatible with noise levels and range compatibility zones associated with military aviation range operations.

(8) Range Compatible Use Zones (RCUZ) Studies identify land uses compatible with noise levels and range compatibility zones associated with military aviation range and military ground range operations.

(9) Joint Land Use Study (JLUS) Program is a cooperative land planning effort between military installations and surrounding communities sponsored by DOD OEA that promotes community growth and development compatible with the training and operational mission of the military installation.

e. Submission Requirements

(1) The timing and format for submission of support requirements will be detailed in an annual data call.

(2) All projects for each installation will be consolidated for submission. Each installation will identify a single point of contact for the submission. Installations must ensure thorough review of cost estimates prior to submission.

(3) CG, MCIs will review all project requests submitted from individual installations under their respective cognizance and rank projects according to regional priority. Training Commands will submit project requests directly to CMC (LFL).

(4) Real Estate Centrally Managed Program funds may only be used for projects approved by CMC (LFL). Installations must

notify CMC (LFL) immediately if funding for approved projects is later determined excess, the requirement for the project changes or is no longer valid, or changes in cost occur.

　　　　(5) Projects that include software development must be annotated in the project title, and must receive approval via the Marine Corps Functional Area Manager (FAM) and Information Technology (IT) procurement process prior to receiving funding. Hardware and software acquisitions will not be supported from the Real Estate Centrally Managed Program.

APPENDIX A

TERMS OF REFERENCE

1. <u>Purpose</u>. This appendix provides terms of reference for policies and procedures for encroachment control management.

    a. Encroachment, as discussed in this Order, refers to factors that degrade or have the potential to degrade the mission capability of a Marine Corps installation, operational range, training area, associated special use airspace, sea space, radio frequency spectrum and other locations within the white-space where the Marine Corps conducts current and plans future military testing, training and general mission activities.

    b. Encroachment Control, as discussed in this Order, describes current mitigation efforts undertaken by the Marine Corps in conjunction with prevention efforts taken by local, state, regional, and national public and private entities to lessen or prevent training impacts caused by encroachment.

    c. White-space, as discussed in this Order, refers to the area outside installation or range compatibility zones (or study planning areas) that, at any given time, is required by operational or tactical doctrine to meet current and future military mission needs and is not under the management control of the military.

    d. Internal Encroachment, as discussed in this Order, refers to uses of, or limitations imposed on installations, operational ranges, and training areas that are incompatible with current and future military testing, training and general mission activities, caused or exacerbated by decisions internal to the Marine Corps, Department of Navy (DON) or Department of Defense (DOD).

    e. Military Mission Sustainment, as discussed in this Order, refers to the capability and capacity of a military installation, operational range, training area, associated special use airspace, sea space, and radio frequency spectrum allocation to provide realistic operations and training resources suitable for the Marine Corps to fulfill general mission activities such as operations and training activities, research, development, test and evaluation activities, and other significant operational, test and evaluation, maintenance, storage, disposal, or other support functions performed by Marine Corps installations.

APPENDIX B

ENCROACHMENT ISSUES

1. <u>Purpose</u>. This appendix provides the Department of Defense (DOD) Senior Readiness Oversight Council (SROC) identified encroachment issues for the Services to investigate and analyze these various pressures on its installations, operational ranges, and training areas. In addition to the policies and responsibilities for compliance with environmental statutes and regulations, as well as the management of Marine Corps environmental programs described in reference (a), encroachment issues currently used to assess installations, operational ranges, training areas and associated special use airspace encroachments are:

   a. <u>Urban Growth</u>. Incompatible development in close proximity to military installations leads to operational challenges for the installation. Such growth is the root cause of many other encroachment concerns. Aircraft operations have adverse noise and safety implications. Ground training, including direct and indirect fire, also generates noise that can adversely affect the surrounding community. Residential areas and places of public assembly such as schools, churches, restaurants, theaters, and shopping centers, are often incompatible with military activities when located close to military installations and ranges. Public pressure to reduce noise and the residual effects of military training and testing activities and to ensure safety often forces installations and ranges to restrict those operations deemed disturbing to the community. In general, such restrictions are put into place during certain hours or when the activities exceed established noise thresholds or safety criteria.

   b. <u>Airborne Noise</u>. Military readiness activities (e.g., aircraft operations, small and large caliber weapons firing, rocket launches, engineer detonations, and sonic booms) generate noise at installations, under low-level flying routes, and at training and testing ranges. The pivotal issue of noise is the impact or perceived impact of noise on people, animals (both wild and domestic), structures, and land use. The degrees to which there are noise restrictions are directly related to the presence of people, wildlife, and noise-sensitive land near military installations, ranges, and low-level Military Training Routes (MTR).

   c. <u>Endangered Species and Critical Habitat</u>. Military lands provide habitat for more than 300 federally-listed threatened

Enclosure (1)

and endangered species that must be protected under the
Endangered Species Act (ESA), reference (f). Many military
installations and ranges are surrounded by urban development and
often become the only large undeveloped areas available to
support endangered species. At the same time, new weapons
systems are being introduced with increased standoff,
survivability, and lethality capabilities. Improved warfighting
capabilities are allowing for greater dispersion of highly
mobile units possessing longer range firepower. Base
realignment and closure has resulted in the concentration of
units within the continental U.S. at remaining bases.
Additionally, forces previously stationed overseas have been
redeployed to U.S. installations. Thus, environmental concerns
arise as a result of greater use of military ranges and
operating areas in the continental U.S. As land use
restrictions increase in order to protect endangered species,
there is reduced flexibility to use military lands for training
and testing. Changes in the ESA that the Congress enacted in
Section 318 of the National Defense Authorization Act (NDAA) for
Fiscal Year (FY) 2004, reference (g), will improve the
Department's ability to balance the conservation of protected
species and military readiness. The provisions in Section 318
will allow the Department to manage protected species through
the implementation of integrated natural resource management
plans required by Section 101 of reference (h), the Sikes Act,
rather than through the designation of critical habitat.

   d. <u>Air and Land Space Restrictions</u>. DOD requires Special
Use Airspace (SUA) to conduct realistic Marine Air Ground Task
Force (MAGTF) training; weapons employment; and critical testing
and evaluation of future aircraft, weapons, and systems. SUA is
vital to military training and testing but is in conflict with
the growing demands of the deregulated commercial airlines and
general aviation that compete with military aviation activities
for the same airspace. Reference (i), the current Federal
Aviation Administration (FAA) projections for 2025, estimate
that air vehicle operations will increase by two to three times
over current levels, with an estimated economic impact of $30
billion annually. To accommodate this anticipated
transportation demand, a Next Generation Air Transportation
System (NGATS), reference (k), is being developed. In support
of the NGATS Plan, the Century of Aviation Act (Public Law 108-
176), Reference (j), was signed in 2003, establishing the Joint
Planning and Development Office (JPDO) as a joint effort between
the Departments of: Transportation (DOT), Defense (DoD),
Commerce (DOC) and Homeland Security (DHS), National Aeronautics
and Space Administration (NASA), and reference (l), the White
House Office of Science and Technology Policy (OSTP). The NGATS

Plan is intended to accommodate increasing demand, while at the same time ensuring aviation safety and reducing the environmental impact of aviation operations. Key objectives of the NGATS Plan which have the potential to impact current military SUA usage, include: the desire to reduce transit times and increase system predictability; the desire to dynamically re-configure airspace and air traffic flows to minimize the impact of weather and other disruptions; and the desire to enable aviation users to negotiate their flight paths based on real-time information sharing among all Air Transportation System participants. It is anticipated that these constraints will put a premium on the ability of the military to manage SUA in near real-time, and have an ability to dynamically re-configure airspace, when necessary. Moreover, these constraints must be balanced against the increased range and mobility of new and emerging weapons platforms and systems, and the corresponding need for increasing volumes of SUA in which to employ these systems in support of realistic training and testing. Solutions to these issues will require a more integrated FAA/DOD process to increase the efficacy of SUA practices and to sustain military SUA for the future. Lack of required access to sufficiently large contiguous pieces of land to conduct doctrinally sound live fire and maneuver training is the single most critical external constraint facing land-based training. Modernization has increased our combat units' speed, range, and mobility and has dramatically improved the command and control capabilities of commanders. They no longer require line-of-sight, but increasingly rely on technology to employ their units. Energy infrastructure has the potential to increase encroachment pressures on military installations, operational ranges, SUA and training areas through resource use demand, tall structure interference, and ecosystem displacement. Constraints on the availability of training lands and SUA are largely a factor of existing installations' footprints, locations of training areas and military training routes, urban growth, and natural resource conservation requirements.

  e. <u>Unexploded Ordnance and Munitions</u>. Ranges and training areas are critical to DOD's ability to conduct realistic, live-fire training and weapon systems testing. Live-fire is, and will remain, the cornerstone of Service training and testing. Military live-fire training and testing activities by necessity deposit unexploded ordnance (UXO) and munitions constituents onto military lands. Reference (m), the Comprehensive Environmental Response, Compensation, and Liability Act (CERCLA aka SuperFund), reference (n), the Resource Conservation and Recovery Act (RCRA), reference (o) the Clean Water Act (CWA), and reference (p), the Safe Drinking Water Act (SDWA) have

implications for the use of military munitions, to include UXO
and munitions constituents on operational ranges. There is a
growing recognition that the application of these environmental
laws in ways unanticipated or unintended when first enacted can
reduce range access, capacity, availability and capability.
Restrictions on training and testing can increase the extent to
which military readiness is compromised. Furthermore, uncertain
applications and inconsistent enforcement of legislation and
regulation limit DOD's ability to plan, program, and budget for
UXO and munitions compliance.

  f. <u>Radio Frequency Encroachment</u>. With very few
exceptions, training and testing rely heavily on the radio
frequency (RF) spectrum. The RF spectrum is essential for the
operation of national defense systems such as Global Positioning
System (GPS), precision guided munitions, tactical radio relay
communication systems, and air combat training systems. These
systems and emerging technologies are becoming increasingly
complex and data-intensive, resulting in an increased demand for
RF bandwidth. Commercial spectrum uses are increasingly coming
into conflict with military RF requirements. Since 1992, DOD
has lost approximately 27 percent of the total RF spectrum
allocated for aircraft telemetry as a result of congressionally
mandated spectrum reallocations and other regulatory mechanisms
to accommodate commercial devices. The reallocation of this
spectrum and increased commercial RF interference, along with
military system demand for bandwidth, put important training and
testing activities at an increased risk.

  g. <u>Maritime Sustainability</u>. Training and testing at sea
is complicated by the demands of regulatory compliance, which
can adversely affect the ability of U.S. Naval forces to sustain
operations, training exercises, and testing in the maritime
environment. For example, reference (q), the Marine Mammal
Protection Act (MMPA) seeks to "protect from harm" sensitive
habitats and living marine resources such as marine mammals, sea
turtles, and coral reefs. But overly restrictive interpretation
of this goal has inhibited naval readiness activities globally.
For example, regulatory compliance efforts require DOD to
consult with United States Fish and Wildlife Service (USFWS),
the National Marine Fisheries Service (NMFS) or National Oceanic
and Atmospheric Administration (NOAA) Fisheries, and state
regulators when a proposed action may "affect" a protected
resource. The consultation process in turn can result in
stringent restrictions on DOD activities. Such measures
restrict training and testing activities essential to naval
readiness and marginalize the Navy's ability to sustain future
training and testing affiliated with emerging technologies.

Enclosure (1)

Section 319 of reference (g) amended the MMPA by clarifying
definitions, authorizing a national security exemption that can
be invoked by the Secretary of Defense, and requiring the
consideration of the impact of MMPA actions on military
readiness activities. These changes will help the Department
address maritime encroachment issues.

h. Air Quality. Readiness limitations can arise due to
application of reference (r), the Clean Air Act (CAA), to
emissions generated on military installations, operational
ranges and training areas. The two most common concerns are
opacity rules and air conformity requirements. Opacity rules
can restrict or prohibit some training and testing activities,
such as smoke and mounted maneuver training, and can limit fires
prescribed to manage vegetation. Opacity is a sensitive issue
with the public, especially near parks and designated wilderness
areas. Conformity is a requirement that certain emissions not
exceed specific thresholds set by the CAA. The effect of the
conformity rule is substantive because the CAA prohibits
military forces from conducting training and testing unless the
activity emissions remain below set thresholds. Therefore,
opacity and conformity standards may restrict certain training
and testing operations, as well as re-stationing or deploying
new weapons systems in nonattainment areas.

i. Cultural Resources. Military installations,
operational ranges and training areas are subject to the
provisions of federal and state legislation and regulation,
including reference (s), the Native American Grave Protection
and Repatriation Act (NAGPRA), reference (t), the National
Historic Preservation Act (NHPA), and reference (u), the
Archaeological Resources Protection Act (ARPA). These statutes
direct the conservation and preservation of Native American,
European, African/American, and other cultural resources sites.
Military installations, operational ranges and training areas
must accommodate these sites by protecting or mitigating
interference with them according to federal and state compliance
requirements. In some cases, the cultural sites may interfere
with training and testing activities by limiting access to areas
where sites are found. In such cases, range management and
operations must adjust to regulatory compliance by providing
training workarounds and mission capable ranges alternatives.

j. Clean Water. Water quality is an environmentally
sensitive issue for all stakeholders on and near military
installations, operational ranges and training areas. The CWA,
the legislation that regulates discharges of pollutants into the
waters of the United States, gives the Environmental Protection

Agency (EPA) the authority to implement pollution control programs such as setting wastewater and water quality standards. The CWA has direct application to military lands where some munitions constituents, combat force effluents, and other contaminants may discharge into water sources and therefore trigger CWA regulatory compliance. Range management and operations must conduct training and testing in accordance with clean water requirements. Moreover, mission capable ranges must accommodate the CWA by protecting rangeland water and underlying aquifers from contaminants and must structure investment strategies to respond to the influences of new missions and technologies on water quality.

   k. Wetlands. Some military installations, operational ranges and training areas contain wetlands, considered a scarce and valuable natural resource. They are vital fish and wildlife habitats, some surrounded by upland with no apparent surface water outlet. Wetlands are unique ecosystems sensitive to disturbance. The EPA manages wetlands in the Office of Wetlands, Oceans, and Watersheds. Military operations normally avoid using wetlands during tactical operations because they are unsuitable for maneuver warfare. Moreover, because they are protected, they require management attention. Range management and operations must consider the impacts of wetlands on current training and testing and must develop mission capable range strategies to accommodate training and testing requirements for evolving operational missions and emerging technologies.

Enclosure (1)

APPENDIX C

OPERATIONS AND TRAINING CONSTRAINTS

1. Purpose. This appendix provides the operations and training
constraints associated with encroachment. The operations and
training constraints summarized and defined in this Order
represent the quantification of the encroachment sources defined
in congressional reports. This degradation or elimination of
certain operations and training activities on installations,
operational ranges, training areas and associated special use
airspace may impact the overall mission and readiness of the
Marine Corps. Such constraints:

     a. Create avoidance areas. Avoidance areas on
installations or ranges are unavailable for training or
operations permanently or temporarily. For example, ground
troops may not be able to train in certain areas due to the
presence of endangered species, or aircraft may have to avoid
certain areas to limit noise. Avoiding these areas can degrade
the quality of training.

     b. Reduce usage days. Operations and training is
restricted or prohibited on some days in some areas. For
example, ships may not be able to operate in certain areas at
specified times because of migrating marine life. Aircraft
training may be prohibited at certain times to avoid migratory
birds or to avoid interfering with the mating season of certain
species.

     c. Prohibit certain operations and training events. For
example, ground troops may be prohibited from digging into the
ground to create realistic fighting positions, aircraft may be
prohibited from using flares or chaff, and ships may be
prohibited from using sonar equipment. In these cases, the
training must be conducted at other locations, or workarounds
must be developed.

     d. Reduce range access. Encroachment can reduce access to
ranges. For example, the approaches to target areas might be
limited to certain specified corridors, rather than access being
permitted from multiple approaches. Such limitations may
degrade the realism and value of the training event.

     e. Segment training and reduce realism. Encroachment may
mean that training events that should naturally follow in
sequence, to mirror their occurrence in combat, might have to be

segmented in training. For example, aircraft might have to practice ordnance delivery and evasive maneuvers at different times, rather than together. Ground forces might have to practice ship-to-shore maneuvers at one time and assaults on enemy positions at another. Segmentation of training reduces realism and the value of training experiences.

   f.   Limits application of new technologies. Concerns about encroachment may limit training or testing with new technologies. For example, encroachment may limit the military's ability to conduct realistic testing or training with unmanned aerial systems, which are now a standard capability on the battlefield. Limitations on testing could very well translate into limited applications in combat, as forces apply technologies as they have in training, and perhaps not to the technology's full potential.

   g.   Restrict flight altitudes. Incompatible development on the ground and demand for air access may prevent military forces from taking full advantage of existing special use airspace or special use airspace development needed to address future requirements. In training, aircraft may be forced to fly at artificially low or high altitudes, which reduces realism and may cause pilots to adapt practices that must be "unlearned" in actual combat.

   h.   Inhibit new tactics development. By restricting maneuver areas, approaches to targets, altitudes, and certain technologies, the creative development of new tactics might be limited.

   i.   Complicate night and all-weather operations and training. The ability to conduct military operations at night and in bad weather is an advantage in combat. Nighttime operations and training, therefore, are essential to force readiness. Nighttime, however, is also the time when residents near military installations, operational ranges and training areas are especially sensitive to noise. Voluntary or mandatory restrictions on military training at night, therefore, may foster better community relations, but they pose especially critical limits on realistic training.

   j.   Reduce live-fire proficiency. Encroachment from continued population growth, increased levels of environmental regulations, and incompatible development around military installations, operational ranges, and training areas reduce opportunities for the use of live-fire ordnance, thereby reducing proficiency. While the use of simulation and inert ordnance can replace some live-fire training, training with live ordnance remains essential for adequately preparing military forces for combat.

1. Increase personnel tempo. Personnel tempo, as discussed in this Order, refers to the amount of time a member of the armed forces is engaged in their official duties at a location or under circumstances that make it infeasible for a member to spend off-duty time in the housing in which the member resides at the member's permanent duty station. Encroachment increases the length of time personnel experience away from their home station when forces must deploy to receive effective training not available locally.

m. Increase costs or risks. Encroachment can increase costs in a variety of ways. Examples include transportation and other costs for units to train away from their home station when encroachment limits training locally or increased fuel costs for aircraft training missions that must be aborted because of encroachments in target areas.

www.ingramcontent.com/pod-product-compliance
Lightning Source LLC
Chambersburg PA
CBHW080623290526
45790CB00007B/2894